14,287 Pieces of Fabric

and Other Poems

Written and Illustrated by

Jean Ray Laury

C&T PUBLISHING

©1994 by Jean Ray Laury

All poems and illustrations by Jean Ray Laury.

Illustration photography by Sharon Risedorph.

Editing by Louise Owens Townsend.

Technical editing by Joyce Engels Lytle.

Design and production by Bobbi Sloan Design, Berkeley, California.

Published by C & T Publishing, P.O. Box 1456, Lafayette, California 94549.

ISBN 0-914881-75-2

Library of Congress Cataloging-in-Publication Data

Laury, Jean Ray,
        14,287 pieces of fabric and other poems / by Jean Ray Laury;
    illustrations by Jean Ray Laury. —1st ed.
            p.   cm.
        ISBN 0-914881-75-2
        1. Quilting—Poetry. 2. Quilts—Poetry. 3. Women—Poetry.
    I. Title.   II. Title: Fourteen thousand two hundred eighty-seven
    pieces of fabric and other poems.
    PS3562.A8433A16   1994
    811'.54—dc20   93-34220
                                                CIP

The Color-Aid papers used in the illustrations were provided by Richard O'Brien at Color Aid Corporation, New York City.

Printed in Hong Kong
First Edition

10   9   8   7   6   5   4   3   2   1

Dedication

To a few of my special friends whose wit and intelligence have sustained me for years. I have never had to explain anything to them (though they listened when I did) and have never had to add "I was kidding." I like them especially because, after all these years, they still like me.

To Beth Gutcheon, whose irrepressible humor plus her total and resolute support have been a highlight of my years in quilting.

To Ruth Milliken Law, a friend since college days, whose remarkable and penetrating wit have illuminated the world in a delightful way.

To Mary Sprague, a friend since graduate school, whose sense of the ridiculous has been a godsend. Her talents and success as a "real" artist and teacher are an inspiration.

To Joyce Aiken, my long-time (33 years!) friend and colleague, whose good-natured giggles know none of the conventional boundaries.

To Jody House, whom I met when she invited me, sight unseen, to stay in her home. That trusting nature, coupled with quick wit and quilting expertise, make her a special friend.

To my daughter Liz Laury, my most honest and insightful critic, whose belief in what I do is always heartwarming.

Acknowledgments

I appreciate the support of the entire C & T staff, and especially Diane Pedersen for her special insights. Editor Louise Townsend is always a pleasure to work with. (And will probably remove the preposition with which I have ended that sentence!) *[Editor's Note: Ah, well, a poet may place a preposition anywhere she needs it!]* Special thanks to Bobbi Sloan, the book's designer, and to Sharon Pilcher for all of her help.

Preface

If you offered me the choice between a book of humorous poems or a toad, I'd probably opt for the toad. Funny verses do not sound particularly appealing to me.

So why am I offering them to you? Well, partly because I'm the helpless victim. I can't quit writing them. It's like running downhill too fast. You can't possibly stop; you can only determine the direction. But I can't quit writing them because each poem offers me some insight or new perspective. Or some tiny absurd aspect of my quilting life is illuminated.

I also offer the poems because you've indicated that you enjoy them. Your responses have overwhelmed me. At the North Carolina Quilt Symposium, a standing ovation followed "Quilting Down at the Old Folks' Home." At the Vermont Quilt Festival, the applause after "14,287 Pieces of Fabric" was thunderous, and I was greatly touched and pleased when the entire audience stood. (At least a few must share my creaking joints. Standing up isn't all that easy!) At the National Quilt Symposium in South Africa, the response was the same. My mailbox has been stuffed with requests and pleas for copies.

So here they are. I had a wonderful time writing them. If they bring you half the pleasure they have brought me, I'll consider it a triumph.

What I like about doing the poems and the illustrations is that they keep me laughing—at me, at myself as a quilter. And—well, OK—at all of us as quilters. Perhaps one of the most endearing qualities of quilters is that they are not overly serious; rarely are they long-faced and grim, or so filled with ponderous solemnity that they can't chuckle convulsively over nonsense.

This book is a natural new direction for my working (or playing) with words, on paper as well as in my quilts. Illustrating is as much fun as writing. Drawing requires that one strips things to their essence, selecting only those parts that further the intended effect. It is still composition, and the elements remain the same, whether it's writing or designing. Repetition, emphasis, pattern, line, rhythm, shape—these are always present, whether one is planning a garden, making a quilt, setting the table, or writing a poem.

Sometimes I did these illustrations by cutting directly into paper. Other times, I first made a sketch, which then guided my cutting. I worked with colored paper, scissors, and paste, using much the same approach as I would with appliqué.

The ideas for the verses come from all of you who have talked to me in or out of class. My models for the drawings are all of the quilters I have ever observed. Knowing that poems would appeal to a small (though select!) portion of the quilt world, I was overwhelmed and delighted when C & T decided to publish this book. It is an act of utter faith on their part. It is a great gift to me and a privilege to be given free rein with the illustrations and the poems. What a pleasure and what a luxury. I love it.

Creating the poems and illustrations gave me great pleasure. I hope you will enjoy them too. They are for you.

Table of Contents

14,287 Pieces of Fabric

Behind the painted picket gate
There lived a quilter known as Kate.

She had one son, a boy named John;
One daughter, whom she doted on.

She had one husband and one house,
One pup, one cat, one little mouse.

And 14,287 pieces of fabric.

And one day her dear husband said
"I need a piece of fabric. Red.

I'll tie it on to this long board
I've got to haul in my old Ford.

Keep sewing, dear, and I'll go find
The piece I need. I know what kind."

"Oh no," she cried "That just won't do.
I'll look myself, and I'll go through

The 14,287 pieces of fabric."

"Now here's a red," said husband Joe.
"It'd be just right." But Kate said "No,

That red is hard to find, you see,
And this red's from my sewing bee.

That's my Denver calico
And this one's from the Houston show.

I've saved this crimson piece for years.
It's much more rare than it appears.

And not THAT one," our Katie cried.
"That turkey red's been set aside.

My sister gave me this bright hue.
Could you use green instead? Or blue?

Oh, dear, I'm sorry I can't share.
There's not a single red to spare

In the 14,287 pieces of fabric."

So Joe went through his closet shelf
And found a piece of red himself.

He took his new red shirt outside
And said, "We're goin' for a ride."

He tied the sleeve around the board,
Secured it with a bungee cord,

And muttered as he drove away,
"Well red is red, that's all I say.

Will wonders never ever cease?
She couldn't find a single piece

In all her 14,287 pieces of fabric."

Then Suzie (she's the little girl)
Slammed through the door, her eyes awhirl.

"I'm hurt. I think I broke my head."
Alarm across her face was spread.

"I need a sling to fix it right
And bandages. They should be white.

I'll find them, Mom. White's all the same.
You needn't leave your quilting frame."

But Kate cried, "Stop! That's not the way!
You'll have to wait for my okay.

Here's one…Oh, no, we can't use it—
I see there's just a tiny bit.

This four-yard length would never do;
I wouldn't want it cut in two.

Here's white I picked up in Vermont.
It's one I know I'm going to want.

I bought this white in Monterey,
And that's my only whitish gray.

This white is from a baby dress,
And dear, oh dear, I must confess.

10

There's nothing here that you can use.
I have no choice. I must refuse."

Poor Suzie stomped her feet and cried,
"I'm injured, and I could have died!"

She took the pillow off her bed
And used the case to bind her head.

From stacks of cloth spread all around,
Not one spare white was ever found

In all the 14,287 pieces of fabric.

Then John (who was her second child)
Came rushing in. His eyes were wild.

"Oh, Mama, help! Emergency!
The grass has caught on fire you see.

We need some cloth to beat the flame.
I played with matches. I'm to blame.

Don't you get up. Just sew away.
I'll grab some cloth and save the day."

"Wait, wait, oh, wait," his mama cried.
"I'll get the cloth." And then she tried

To find some blue she'd never sew,
But not THAT blue. Nor this one, no.

"Well maybe there's a yukky green.
I'm sure that somewhere I have seen

A color I would never use.
But how to choose? Oh, how to choose?

Oh, here's my gramma's yellow print
And springtime colors, pink and mint,

Plus bits from babies' tiny bibs
And lots of quilt scraps from the cribs.

And lavenders and turquoise blue,
Lime green and orange, hue on hue.

Some fabric from the guild exchange
And prints in an extensive range.

And, oh, my dear, it's sad but true.
There is no fabric here for you."

John raised his arms and tore his hair
And shouted "Mama, don't you care?"

Well, John could see the flames by then.
He called the fire department men

Who came and doused the flames at last
While mama talked about the past

And searched the fabrics on her lap,
But never found a single scrap

That she could share or give or lend
To save their home from dreadful end,

In all the 14,287 pieces of fabric.

That night they all sat down to rest
And watched the sun sink in the west.

The old porch swing went to and fro
With passengers, both Kate and Joe.

While on one arm sat little John,
And Suzie with her nightie on.

The night grew dark, the air was still.
It soon cooled off and then grew chill.

John shivered in the chilly breeze,
And Suzie was the first to sneeze.

Then Kate and Joe both went "Ahchoo!"
"Ahchoo!" went John and Suzie, too.

They shook and shivered, coughed and wheezed;
They blew their noses, and they sneezed.

Then Kate leaped up and cried, "Indeed!
I know exactly what you need.

12

You need one great big quilt that goes
All over you from head to toes,

That stretches over this whole swing
And covers nearly everything."

She ran inside. She cleared a space.
She turned the lights on every place.

She got her cutting board, her tools,
Her scissors, templates, plastic rules,

Some pens (in disappearing blue)
Her board, and then her steam iron too.

Thimbles, coffee, colored thread,
Batting, pins, and then she said,

"Things are ready. I'm all set.
All I need to do is get

My 14,287 pieces of fabric."

Kate was like a thing possessed.
She worked with speed and joy and zest.

She worked 'til nine and then half past.
At ten she said, "It's going fast."

13

She worked right past the midnight chime
'Til one, oblivious of time.

She cut and pinned 'til very late.
But time did not exist for Kate.

The hour was three and later four,
And Kate could hear her husband's snore.

"It's great," said Kate. "I'm sewing fast.
I'll use up all my scraps at last…

All 14,287 pieces of fabric."

She cut and sewed from five to six
And then at eight she stopped to fix

A pot of tea, both hot and strong,
To help the stitches move along.

At nine she said to Joe, "My dear,
Please fix the toast. I'm outta here."

She needed just a bit of brown
And said, "I'll check the shop in town."

At just ten thirty she was back
With five large bags and one huge sack.

"I found a bit of yellow-green
And violet (the best I've seen),

A new cerise, a midnight blue,
Some stripes and plaids, an olive hue,

A forest green, a pink (quite hot),
And truly, that was all I got."

"But oh," said Kate, with one big frown.
"I totally forgot the brown."

Then down she sat to sew some more
Through noon, and one and two and four.

By five she said "It's very clear
That six will see the end quite near."

She sewed the borders on and then
The binding last, at 7:10.

The quilt was done by half past eight.
She signed her name and wrote the date.

And by the time the air grew chill
Kate's fingers, finally, were still.

She gathered up the work she'd done
And went to watch the setting sun.

Out on the swing sat Joe and John
And Suzie with her nightie on.

"Look here," said Kate. "Surprise, surprise!
I've made a quilt to feast your eyes,

To warm your toes, to banish chill
To keep those shaking shivers still."

"It's beautiful," they cried. "It's great.
The nicest quilt in this whole state."

They snuggled in. They wrapped up tight.
The old porch swing was quite a sight.

As Kate leaned back to rest her head
"I used so many scraps," she said.

"Almost all of my 14,287 pieces of fabric."

From Kate we heard not one more peep
For she was shortly sound asleep.

They covered her with tender care
And said, "We'll let her sleep right there."

17

18

While on the swing our Katie snoozed.
She dreamed of fabrics she had used,

Envisioned colors it would take
For all the quilts she planned to make.

And in her dreams she sewed so fast
She used up all her cloth at last!

All 14,287 pieces of fabric.

The Lap Quilter

A dear young divorcee named Myrt
Cut some squares from her ex-husband's shirt.
When he came to collect it,
He found that she'd wrecked it
And quilted his shirt to her skirt.

19

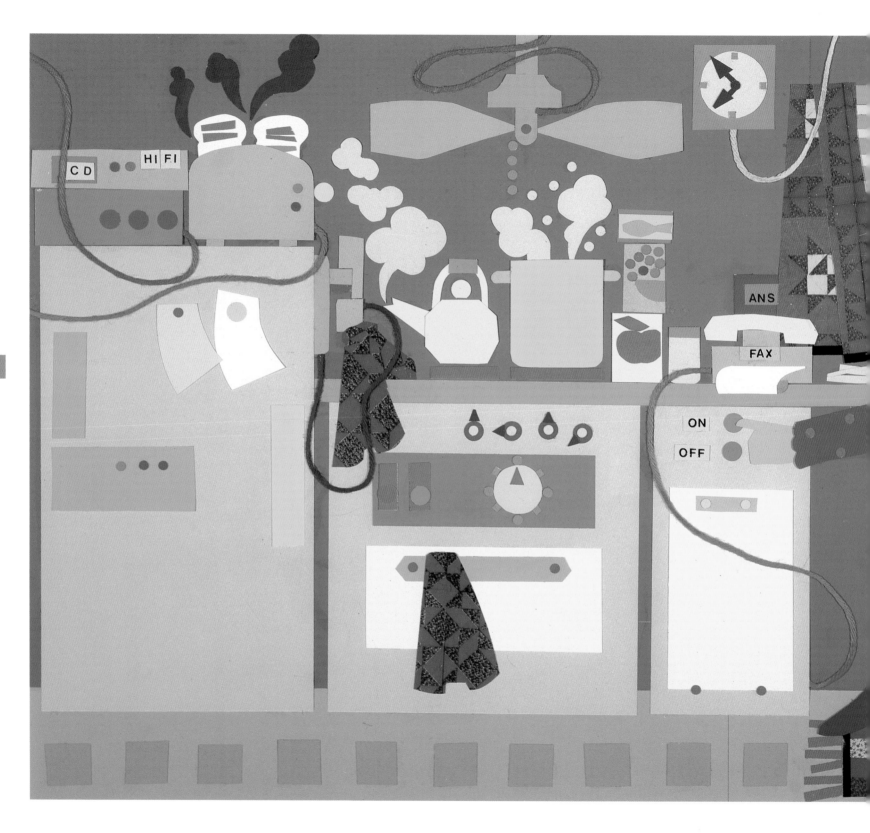

The Efficient Home-maker

Lilly has a freezer
That defrosts all by itself.
Her meals in frozen packages
Are on the freezer shelf.

Her oven is self-cleaning,
And she has a washer-dryer,
Electric knives and mixers,
And an automatic fryer.

She revels in her microwave,
Which cooks her meals with speed.
It has a fast-defroster
Just in case there is a need.

22

"I'm really very modern,"
Says our modest little Lilly.
"Old-fashioned ways take too much time,
And some are even silly.

"I do not cook at all the way
My granny used to do.
I push a button here or there
And turn a knob or two."

"You save a lot of time, I'm sure,"
Said Lilly's next door neighbor.

"You must have hours of leisure
Since you save on household labor.

"So tell me how you use the time,
And what you do instead."
And Lilly said, "I piece the quilts
To spread out on my bed."

"Oh my," her neighbor said. "You must
Have all the latest means.
The newest model over-lock
Computerized machines.

"And stitches that are activated
By a voice command,
A quilting foot, a walking foot
And patterns on demand.

"I'll bet it winds your bobbins,
And it cuts the thread in two.
The feed dogs drop, the cord retracts
Whenever you are through."

"Oh no," said Lilly quite surprised.
"You just don't understand.
I save the time just so that I
Can sew my quilts by hand."

To Cathy, Who Upholds the Highest Housekeeping Standards of Cleanliness and Care

"I'm crazy," said Cathy, "to get to my quilt."
But she looked at her house and was stricken with guilt.
    So she went room to room
    With her mop and her broom,
And she never, no never, quite got to her quilt.

Farmer John and the Miraculous Quilt

Good Farmer John had mowed the hay.
He'd plowed and worked and hoed all day.
He harvested the beans and corn.
His muscles ached; his jeans were torn.

His payment on the land was due
In just another week or two.
He labored hard for every dime
To make his payment right on time.

The landlord (Mr. Cash) did say
"The money's due…you've got to pay
Or I will confiscate this farm."
Good Farmer John expressed alarm.

The frosts were hard. The rains were late.
And Farmer John did fear his fate.
Exhausted, he came in at noon
And called "Hey, Liz. Is lunch on soon?

28

"I'm hungry, and I want to eat.
I need potatoes, corn, and meat."
But Liz was nowhere to be seen.
Said John, "Whatever can this mean?"

He found her with her cloth and thread
"I'm sewing on my quilt," she said.
"There's peanut butter in the jar,
And maybe there's a candy bar.

"But don't disturb me! Let me sew!
I've got to make my quilt, you know."
So John went to the kitchen shelf
And found some lunch all by himself.

At dark, poor Farmer John came in.
"What's this?" he cried. "Cold food ag'in?"
And Liz, oblivious to guilt,
Just answered as she stitched her quilt:

"Our guild exhibit's coming soon.
I must be through by Wednesday noon."
She quilted late into the night.
The moon went down; the sky grew light.

She wearily crawled into bed,
And to her husband John she said,
"Good night," and much to her surprise,
He said, "Good morning. Time to rise."

She worked through breakfast, lunch, and tea,
And quilted on relentlessly.
She cooked no meat nor fowl nor fish
And never washed a single dish.

For days she kept herself indoors
Ignoring things like dirty floors.
The milk went sour; the cat grew lean.
The laundry basket was obscene.

30

Poor Farmer John said, "Well, I see
That Liz has quite forgotten me.
She has no interest in our home
Or food or farm or telephone."

And then on Wednesday, just at noon,
Her quilt was finished—none too soon.
The show was hung in Quilters' Hall
Adjacent to the village mall.

The auction started right at nine,
With Liz among the first in line.
And when her quilt went on the block,
Dear Liz was in for quite a shock.

The bidder waving his right arm
Was Cash, the landlord of the farm.
The bids flew back and forth quite fast,
But Mr. Cash won out at last.

He'd heard that quilts were really hot
And thought that he should buy a lot,
Then sell them to some City Slick
And make a bunch of money quick.

"So if I choose with any luck
I'll make a quick and easy buck."
Liz heard the shouting auctioneer
Cry, "Going, Going, Gone!" quite clear.

The money owed to Liz was due.
Said Cash, "I'll pay by I.O.U."
Then Liz ran home; her heart beat fast.
Her secret plan had worked at last.

When landlord Cash next came to call
He said, "Pay up! Or lose it all!"
He licked his lips; he rubbed his hands,
Anticipating added lands.

"The final payment I'll collect
Or, Farmer John, your plans are wrecked."
"Oh, drat," said John. "I see no way
To get this payment made today."

Then Liz came in and standing tall
Said, "Here it is. I have it all."
The landlord stuttered in defeat.
He clenched his fists and stamped his feet.

He then begrudgingly withdrew,
Departing with his I.O.U.
And Farmer John said, "I'm amazed.
I'm overcome. I'm simply dazed."

He tied an apron 'round his jeans
And learned to fix the corn and beans.
He put his hand to mop and broom
Then built (for Liz) a sewing room.

And when the landlord's luck was down
Old Farmer John drove into town,
And bought the quilt that Liz had sewn
So he could have it for his own.

He hung it on the kitchen wall
Where he announced to one and all
That if you listen to your wife,
Quilting may just change your life.

The Art Quilter

She was at her machine every morning
And she sat at her frame every night.
She stitched and she sewed
As her eyes simply glowed
For all of it gave her delight.

Then her husband brought in his torn trousers,
Saying, "Look, now my cheek's peeking through.
Just make a quick patch
In a blue that will match,
And my pants will be good as when new.

"I know you're an expert at sewing,
Your serger and you make a team.
And all that I ask
Is this one little task.
You can do it with one minor seam."

Then her eyes grew as wide as big saucers
And she said, with her hand to her brow:
"Oh, this is offending!
An artist do mending?
I haven't a clue as to how."

Quilting Down at the Old Folks' Home

37

For at least 50 years
(Maybe more, I've been told)
Diana had lived
In a house up the road.

Diana made quilts
That were simply exquisite
But one day (at home)
She received an odd visit.

In front of her house
Parked a big yellow van
And from it emerged
A blue-uniformed man.

"Department of Health
Calling, Ma'am," he then said.
"Your neighbors were worried.
They thought you were dead.

"You're not taking very good
Care of yourself.
Buying fabrics, not groceries.
You'll ruin your health.

"You stay up all night,
And the others have seen
That you're constantly at
Your infernal machine.

"The rest home will put
A big smile on your face.
You'll like it, Diana;
It's your kind of place."

Diana said, "Well,
Let me pack up some clothes."
While she looked all about
And then carefully chose

Her scissors and needles,
Her patterns and thread,
Her infernal machine,
And a quilt for her bed.

Off to Peace and Hope Manor
They sped in the van.
The neighbors all waved
To departing Diane.

They transferred her cloth,
Her machine, and her chair.
She cried, "Head for the sitting room.
Put my stuff there."

It took her exactly
One night and two days
To involve all the people
In various ways.

All the fabrics were cut up
And pieced into blocks.
The colors and patterns
Would knock off your socks.

The men loved the cutting;
The women could stitch.

They all worked together
To quilt "in the ditch."

When they ran out of fabric,
The curtains were used.
Said the staff at the rest home,
"We are not amused."

They cut up their napkins.
Pajamas went next;
Then nighties while Nursie
Grew dangerously vexed.

"Oh stop it," she shouted.
"Don't strip this place down.
We'll buy you some cloth
At that shop in the town."

They stripped the new cloth,
And they pieced, and they tacked
Until every last senior
Got into the act.

Clair, who'd been silent
Since first moving in
Hollered, "Take out that yellow;
It's ugly as sin."

Eduardo, who scarcely
Ate even a bite
Developed, from sewing,
A huge appetite.

Then George who'd done nothing
But wheedle and whine
Bellowed, "Wait, I can do
Geometric design."

Priscilla who stayed in her
Room day and night
Came out shouting, "Hold on there!
Let me do it right."

Three crutches were tossed.
Some arthritis diminished.
The aches and pains vanished
As quilt tops were finished.

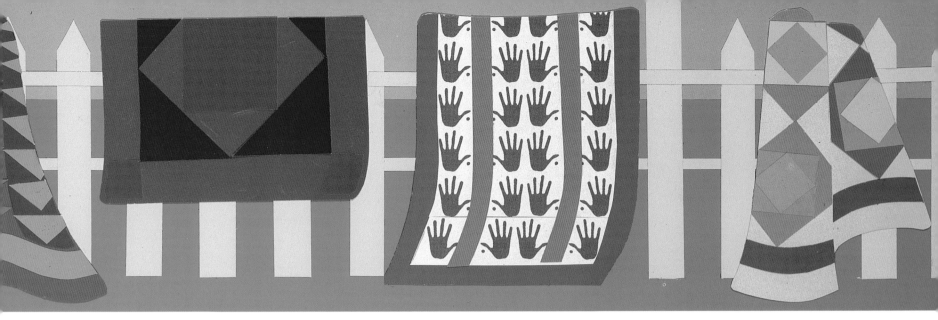

Diana was in her full
Glory by then.
The number of quilts
They had finished was ten.

And when they'd completed
A dozen or two
Diana said, "Let's put them
All out on view."

So over the pickets
At Peace and Hope Manor
Each quilt made a brilliant
And colorful banner.

Three visitors came
From the local museum.
They'd heard of the quilts,
And they wanted to see 'em.

"Astonishing! Simply
Fantastic!" they said.
"But they're too avant garde
To be used on a bed."

"Remarkable juxtapositions
Of view,
The abstract conceptions
Are totally new.

"Perfect originals!
Marvelous minds!
Like Warhol and Diebenkorn:
One-of-a-kinds.

"We'll have an exhibit;
They're bound to say yes.
What they'd do with artwork
I really can't guess.

"How could they refuse us.
They're in no position.
Why, we'll even give them
A little commission."

Then Ethel said, "Hold it.
These quilts aren't for you.
We made them. We like them.
And we'll use them too."

Diane led all of the
Ladies and gents
Out to pick up their quilts
From the white picket fence.

Back to Peace and Hope Manor
They trudged with their quilts
Immersed, as they were, in them
Up to their hilts.

The quilts were all wrapped
Over wheelchairs and knees,
On sofas and beds
And the porch, if you please.

The quilts came to rest
In the very best place.
You can tell by the size
Of the smile on each face.

Now all of Diana's
Old neighbors and friends
And all of the people
The museum sends

Can come to the Manor
To pay a good visit
And view the new quilts,
Which are simply exquisite.

Aerobics at the Quilting Frame

"Be sure to get your exercise,
Make sure you're keeping fit.
When you go to your quilting frame,
Then all you do is sit."

And thus did Bill admonish Bets
To keep her youthful vigor.
"Go several miles each day," he said,
"And keep your girlish figger."

"Why I sew seven miles a day,
And quilt another five.
This constant exercise," said Bets
"Is what keeps me alive."

Then Bill said, "You should lift some weights
To keep you in good health."
"I do! I do! I lift my cloth
Right up onto the shelf.

"And then I also lift my fork,
And lift my cup of tea.

Eight ounces forty times a day
Soon makes two tons, or three.

"I lift a goodly chunk of weight
As I rise for a snack,
And burn off all the calories
By walking briskly back.

"The stitching is aerobic and,
Of course, I also run.
Right up the aisles between the bolts;
Good exercise is fun!"

And Bets said, "Broadness at the beam
Gives force to all my quilting.
And weight provides reserves that will
Prevent unwanted wilting.

"So don't you worry, Bill," said Bets.
"On health I'm nearly phobic.
For quilting, I am quite convinced,
Is naturally aerobic."

Needles and Pins

As a quilter, young Jill can't be beat.
Her work's innovative and neat.
But among her few sins
She drops needles and pins,
Which her husband then finds with his feet.

46

About the Author

The popularity of Jean Ray Laury's classes is a tribute to her ability to encourage and inspire others. She is quiet, humorous, and very professional in her work. Her lectures, among the favorites at conferences and festivals over four continents, are insightful, funny, and full of information.

Jean's B.A. degree in Art and English (University of Northern Iowa) and her M.A. in Design (Stanford University) prepared her for a career of teaching and free-lance design work. Among her books most familiar to quiltmakers are: *Imagery on Fabric; No Dragons on My Quilt* (a children's book); *Incredible Quilts for Kids; Ho for California! Pioneer Women and Their Quilts; The Creative Woman's Getting-It-All-Together Handbook; The Adventures of Sunbonnet Sue;* and several others.

Jean is known for her original quilts, many of which include words and messages supportive of women and quilters. Women's and arts organizations have recognized her accomplishments, and her work has been exhibited in museums and galleries. Private residences and museums as well as public and corporate offices include her work in their collections.

Jean's home and studio are in the foothills of the California Sierra where she enjoys the woods, her family, hiking, reading, and eating, but not necessarily in that order.

47

Other Fine Quilting Books From C & T Publishing

Appliqué 12 Easy Ways! Elly Sienkiewicz

The Art of Silk Ribbon Embroidery, Judith Montano

The Best From Gooseberry Hill: Patterns For Stuffed Animals & Dolls, Kathy Pace

Christmas Traditions From the Heart, Margaret Peters

Crazy Quilt Handbook, Judith Montano

Crazy Quilt Odyssey, Judith Montano

Design a Baltimore Album Quilt! Elly Sienkiewicz

Dimensional Appliqué—Baskets, Blooms & Baltimore Borders, Elly Sienkiewicz

Isometric Perspective, Katie Pasquini-Masopust

The Magical Effects of Color, Joen Wolfrom

Mastering Machine Appliqué, Harriet Hargrave

NSA Series: Bloomin' Creations; Holiday Magic; Hometown; Fans, Hearts, & Folk Art, Jean Wells

Pattern Play, Doreen Speckmann

PQME Series: Milky Way Quilt; Nine-Patch Quilt; Pinwheel Quilt; and *Stars & Hearts Quilt*, Jean Wells

Quilts, Quilts, and More Quilts! Diana McClun and Laura Nownes

Recollections, Judith Montano

Stitching Free: Easy Machine Pictures, Shirley Nilsson

A Treasury of Quilt Labels, Susan McKelvey

Visions: The Art of the Quilt, Quilt San Diego

Whimsical Animals, Miriam Gourley

For more information write for a free catalog from
C & T Publishing
P.O. Box 1456
Lafayette, CA 94549
1-800-284-1114